THIS BOOK BELONGS TO

_____

Don't miss the picture books
in Marcus Pfister's bestselling
Rainbow Fish series:

The Rainbow Fish
Rainbow Fish to the Rescue!
Rainbow Fish and the Big Blue Whale

First published in the United States, Great Britain, Canada,
Australia, and New Zealand in 1999 by North-South Books,
an imprint of Nord-Süd Verlag AG, Gossau Zürich, Switzerland.

Distributed in the United States by North-South Books Inc., New York.

ISBN 0-7358-1110-5
1 3 5 7 9 10 8 6 4 2
Printed in Italy

For more information about our books, and the authors and artists
who create them, visit our web site: http://www.northsouth.com

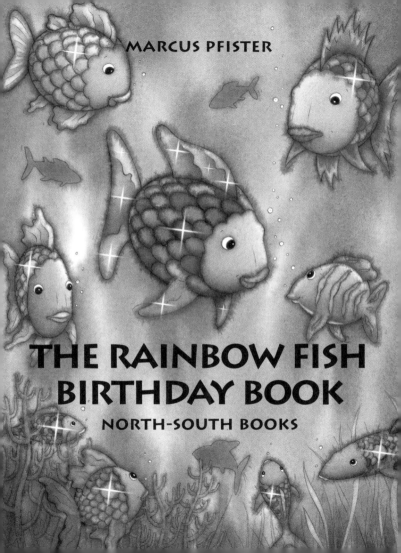

JANUARY

1

2

3

4

5

JANUARY

6

7

8

9

10

JANUARY

11

JANUARY

12

13

14

15

16

JANUARY

17 _____

_____

_____

18 _____

_____

_____

19 _____

_____

_____

20 _____

_____

_____

21 _____

_____

_____

22 _____

_____

23 _____

_____

24 _____

_____

25 _____

_____

26 _____

_____

JANUARY

27

28

29

30

31

JANUARY

FEBRUARY

1_____

_____

_____

2_____

_____

_____

3_____

_____

_____

4_____

_____

_____

5_____

_____

_____

FEBRUARY

6

7

8

9

10

FEBRUARY

11

12

13

14

15

FEBRUARY

16

17

18

19

20

FEBRUARY

21

22

23

24

25

FEBRUARY

26

27

28

29

FEBRUARY

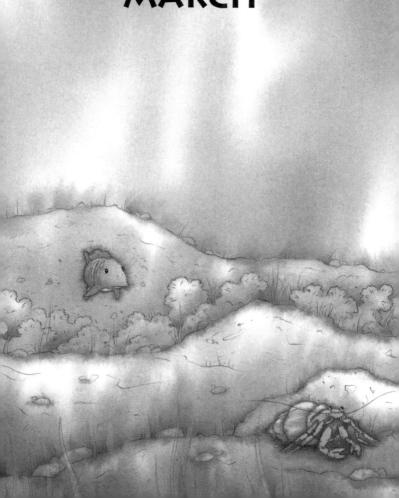

MARCH

1

2

3

4

5

MARCH

6

7

8

9

10

MARCH

11

12

13

14

15

MARCH

16

MARCH

17

18

19

20

21

MARCH

22

23

24

25

26

MARCH

27

28

29

30

31

MARCH

APRIL

1_____

_____

_____

2_____

_____

_____

3_____

_____

_____

4_____

_____

_____

5_____

_____

_____

APRIL

6

7

8

9

10

APRIL

11

12

13

14

15

APRIL

16

17

18

19

20

APRIL

21

22

23

24

25

APRIL

26

27

28

29

30

APRIL

MAY

1_____

_____

_____

2_____

_____

_____

3_____

_____

_____

4_____

_____

_____

5_____

_____

_____

MAY

6 _____

_____

_____

7 _____

_____

_____

8 _____

_____

_____

9 _____

_____

_____

10 _____

_____

_____

MAY

11

12

13

14

15

MAY

16

MAY

17 _____

_____

_____

18 _____

_____

_____

19 _____

_____

_____

20 _____

_____

_____

21 _____

_____

_____

MAY

22 _____

_____

_____

23 _____

_____

_____

24 _____

_____

_____

25 _____

_____

_____

26 _____

_____

_____

MAY

27_____

_____

_____

28_____

_____

_____

29_____

_____

_____

30_____

_____

_____

31_____

_____

_____

MAY

JUNE

1

2

3

4

5

JUNE

6

7

8

9

10

JUNE

11

12

13

14

15

JUNE

16_____

_____

_____

17_____

_____

_____

18_____

_____

_____

19_____

_____

_____

20_____

_____

_____

JUNE

21

22

23

24

25

26

27

28

29

30

JUNE

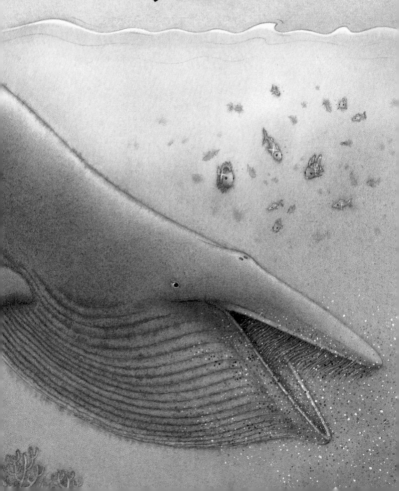

1_____

_____

_____

2_____

_____

_____

3_____

_____

_____

4_____

_____

_____

5_____

_____

_____

JULY

6

7

8

9

10

JULY

11

12

13

14

15

JULY

16

JULY

17

18

19

20

21

JULY

22

23

24

25

26

JULY

27 _____

_____

_____

28 _____

_____

_____

29 _____

_____

_____

30 _____

_____

_____

31 _____

_____

_____

JULY

AUGUST

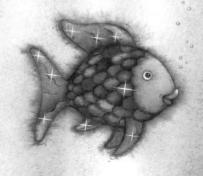

1

2

3

4

5

AUGUST

6

7

8

9

10

AUGUST

11

12

13

14

15

AUGUST

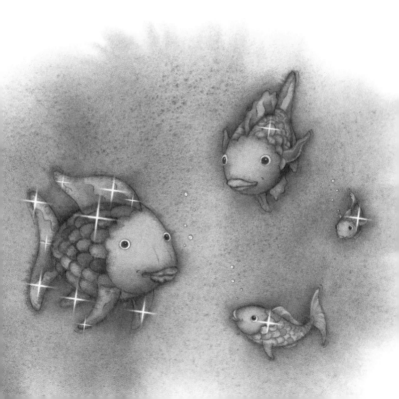

17

18

19

20

21

AUGUST

22

23

24

25

26

AUGUST

27

28

29

30

31

AUGUST

SEPTEMBER

1

2

3

4

5

SEPTEMBER

6

7

8

9

10

SEPTEMBER

11

12

13

14

15

SEPTEMBER

16

17

18

19

20

SEPTEMBER

21

22

23

24

25

SEPTEMBER

26

27

28

29

30

SEPTEMBER

1

2

3

4

5

OCTOBER

6

7

8

9

10

OCTOBER

11

12

13

14

15

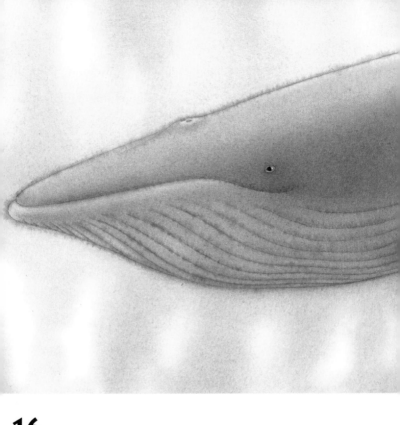

16_____

_____

_____

OCTOBER

17

18

19

20

21

OCTOBER

22 _____

_____

23 _____

_____

24 _____

_____

25 _____

_____

26 _____

_____

OCTOBER

27 _____

_____

_____

28 _____

_____

_____

29 _____

_____

_____

30 _____

_____

_____

31 _____

_____

_____

OCTOBER

NOVEMBER

1_____

_____

2_____

_____

3_____

_____

4_____

_____

5_____

_____

NOVEMBER

6 _____

_____

_____

7 _____

_____

_____

8 _____

_____

_____

9 _____

_____

_____

10 _____

_____

_____

NOVEMBER

11

12

13

14

15

NOVEMBER

16_____

_____

17_____

_____

18_____

_____

19_____

_____

20_____

_____

NOVEMBER

21

22

23

24

25

NOVEMBER

26_____

_____

_____

27_____

_____

_____

28_____

_____

_____

29_____

_____

_____

30_____

_____

_____

NOVEMBER

DECEMBER

1

2

3

4

5

DECEMBER

6

7

8

9

10

DECEMBER

11

12

13

14

15

DECEMBER

16 _____

_____

_____

DECEMBER

17

18

19

20

21

DECEMBER

22

23

24

25

26

DECEMBER

27

28

29

30

31

NOTES

_____

_____

_____

_____

_____

_____

_____

_____

_____

_____